~ DISGUSTING HISTORY ~

GRITTY, STINKY
ANCIENT EGYPT

THE DISGUSTING DETAILS
ABOUT LIFE IN ANCIENT EGYPT

by James A. Corrick

raintree

a Capstone company — publishers for children

Raintree is an imprint of Capstone Global Library Limited, a company incorporated in England and Wales having its registered office at 264 Banbury Road, Oxford, OX2 7DY – Registered company number: 6695582

www.raintree.co.uk
myorders@raintree.co.uk

Edited by Mari Bolte
Designed by Gene Bentdahl
Picture research by Svetlana Zhurkin
Production by Eric Manske

ISBN 978 1 4747 1964 3
19 18 17 16 15
10 9 8 7 6 5 4 3 2 1

British Library Cataloguing in Publication Data
A full catalogue record for this book is available from the British Library

Photo Credits
Alamy: North Wind Picture Archives, 28–29, Paris Pierce, 25; Art Resource, N.Y.: The Trustees of the British Museum, 16, Werner Forman, 23; Artville, 18 (left); The Bridgeman Art Library: Egyptian National Museum, Cairo, Egypt, 27 (top), Index, Barcelona, Spain, 6–7, National Geographic Image Collection, cover, 10–11, 17, Private Collection/Look and Learn, 21, 24; Corbis/Royalty-free, 4 (middle); Getty Images: The Bridgeman Art Library, 9 (top front), De Agostini/G. Dagli Orti, 18–19; iStockphoto: ELENart, 4 (btm left), Goran Bogicevic, 4 (top left), Vladimir Korostyshevskiy, 4 (btm right); Library of Congress, 5 (btm right); Mary Evans Picture Library: 12–13, Illustrated London News, 14–15; Shutterstock: akva, 9 (back), 27 (btm), freelanceartist, grunge design, kmiragaya, 5 (btm left), Turi Tamas, fact box design element

Primary source bibliography
Page 9—from *Ancient Near Eastern Texts Relating to the Old Testament*, edited by James B. Pritchard (Princeton, N.J.: Princeton University Press, 1955) and reprinted in *Everyday Life in Ancient Egypt* by Lionel Casson (Baltimore: Johns Hopkins University Press, 2001).
Page 27—from *Ancient Records of Egypt; Historical Documents from the Earliest Times to the Persian Conquest*, collected, edited, and translated, with commentary by James Henry Breasted. Chicago: The University of Chicago Press, 1906-07).

We would like to thank Jen Houser Wegner, PhD, for her invaluable help in the preparation of this book.

Printed and bound in China

CONTENTS

ANCIENT EGYPT

3100–30 BC

PAGE 9

3100–2700 BC

Narmer unites Upper and Lower Egypt. Memphis is the capital. Writing appears, in the form of hieroglyphs.

2625 BC

The Old Kingdom begins.

THE GREAT PYRAMID: THE NUMBERS

51.710.000 METRIC TONS total weight

23.000.000 approximate number of blocks

2.3 METRIC TONS average weight of one block

13.6 METRIC TONS weight of the largest block

230 METRES (756 FEET) length of the pyramid's base on one side

5.3 HECTARES (13.1 ACRES) total area of the pyramid's base

146.7 METRES (481.3 FEET) the pyramid's original height

PAGE 7

2589–2566 BC

Pharaoh Khufu rules and builds the Great Pyramid at Giza.

2181 BC

The Old Kingdom ends.

MILLIONS OF MUMMIES

It has been estimated that over 70 million mummies were made during the time of the pharaohs.

1550 BC

The New Kingdom begins.

2055 BC

The Middle Kingdom begins. Its capital is Thebes.

1650 BC

The Middle Kingdom comes to an end.

PAGE 26

1650–1550 BC

Hyksos invaders conquer and rule much of Egypt. They bring the chariot to Egypt.

1279–1213 BC

Pharaoh Ramses II rules Egypt.

MEDITERRANEAN SEA

THE CAPITAL
The capital of Egypt has changed many times. Thebes has been the capital four different times. Cairo was not chosen until AD 969.

KEY

— RIVERS

▭ VALLEY OF THE KINGS

☆ CAPITAL CITY

● CITY

0	100 MILES
0	161 KM

N
W ✛ E
S

NILE DELTA

LOWER EGYPT

GIZA ● ● CAIRO

● MEMPHIS

EGYPT

RIVER NILE

VALLEY OF THE KINGS ▭ ☆ **THEBES**

RED SEA

UPPER EGYPT

1069 BC
The New Kingdom comes to an end.

332 BC
Alexander the Great conquers Egypt.

305 BC
The Greek Ptolemaic family becomes Egypt's rulers.

30 BC
Queen Cleopatra VII dies. Rome conquers Egypt.

ANCIENT HISTORY

Ancient Egypt is known for its pyramids, pharaohs and, of course, mummies! But it was also a place where backbreaking labour, deadly illnesses and dirty rivers were common. For about 3,000 years, ancient Egyptians toiled under the hot sun. Pyramids had to be built. Mummies had to be made. And sand from the Sahara desert got in everything.

Ancient Egyptians lived along the banks of the River Nile. The river water was polluted with human and animal waste.

Dangerous animals called the river home, too. Hungry crocodiles lived along the riverbank, waiting for an unsuspecting person or animal to get too close.

During the flooding season, no farming could be done. Instead, the pharaoh required men to build the pyramids. They were not paid. Their work was seen as a service to the pharaoh and his family. Men worked for eight days and then rested for the next two days. Some men were given the day off on special holidays. Others were given time off to work on their own tombs. Leaders liked to keep the peasants busy year-round. They thought that if their subjects were working, there would be less time to get bored and cause trouble.

Nearly 70 pyramids were built around Cairo.

THE WORKING CLASSES

Who's the boss? In ancient Egypt, it was the pharaoh. Most pharaohs were men, but a few were women. The pharaoh was believed to be the earthly form of Horus, the Egyptian sky god.

Apart from the pharaoh and his family, Egyptian society had three main classes. At the top were the rich nobles, who included governors and priests. They owned most of the land and wealth. Below them were artists and educated men. This class included doctors, lawyers, teachers and record keepers called scribes.

The lowest part of society was the working class. More than 80 per cent of the population belonged to the working class. Peasant men worked on farms and in quarries and mines. Women served as dancers, maids or hairdressers.

After the yearly flood, it was the peasants' job to plough, plant and harvest the fields. Some peasants had animals to pull their ploughs, but others had to do it themselves. Preparing fields and harvesting crops was backbreaking work. And a portion of every harvest went directly to the pharaoh as taxes.

Scribes held a high rank in ancient Egypt.

The written word

Be a scribe. More effective is a book than a decorated tombstone… A man is perished, his corpse is dust, all his relatives are come to the ground – (but) it is writing that makes him remembered.

From a writing exercise for apprentices wishing to become scribes.

Some work gangs chipped away in the quarries. Rock from the quarries was used to build the pyramids and other large buildings. Blocks of stone were cut by hand from the quarry floor and walls. These blocks weighed several tons each. The work was slow. The labourers' tools were made from stone or metals such as copper and bronze. Their tools dulled quickly. The soft blades only chipped off very small pieces of rock at a time.

Sometimes workers had to crawl under a stone to free it from the quarry rock. They wiggled into a space only slightly larger than themselves. The only light came from a small oil lamp. The workers breathed in stone dust, which damaged their lungs. And there was always the danger of being crushed by the huge blocks.

Ships carried the stone blocks up or down the Nile. From the ship, large gangs of men used ropes to drag the blocks to the building site. It was hard, sweaty work under the hot Egyptian sun.

Working in the mines was even worse. Workers lay on their stomachs in tight-fitting tunnels and chipped out gold and gems. There was always the danger of being buried alive in a cave-in.

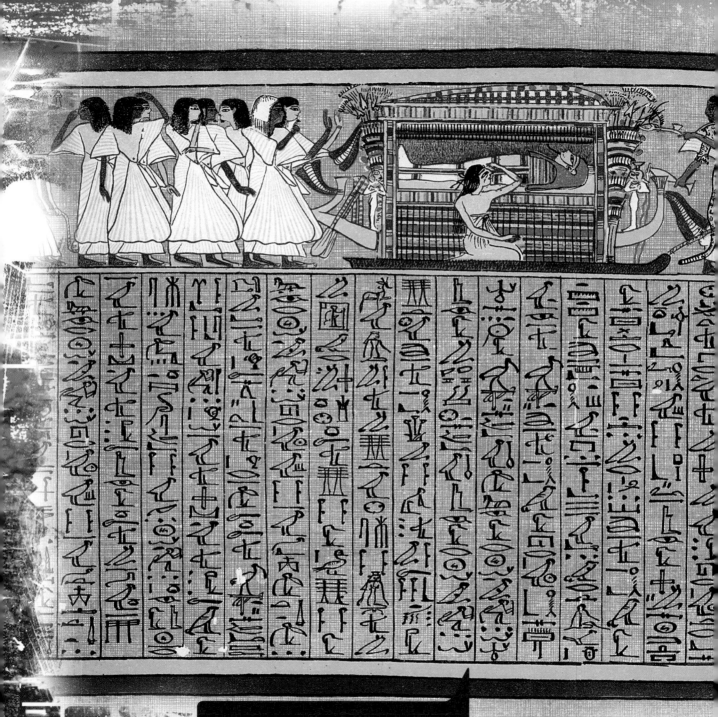

A section of the *Book of the Dead.*

MAKING A MUMMY

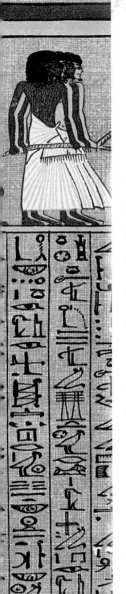

For ancient Egyptians, death was a new beginning. Ancient Egyptians believed in the afterlife. People who died met Osiris, the god of the underworld. Those who passed the god's judgment lived forever. The dead were buried with religious texts and magic spells like those found in the *Book of the Dead*. The spells helped the dead make a successful passage into the afterlife.

The Egyptians believed that the soul of the dead person returned to the physical body from time to time. The body could not be left to rot, or the soul might not recognize it.

Special workers preserved the body through a process called **mummification**. They started by removing the dead person's brain. First, a metal hook was pushed up the body's nose and wiggled around to break up the brain. The brain would drain out while the rest of the body dried. Ancient Egyptians didn't know that the brain was important. To them, the heart was the most important internal organ.

mummification process of making a mummy to preserve a dead person's body

Next, they cleaned out the inside of the body. Workers removed the intestines, liver, stomach and lungs. But they left the heart. Ancient Egyptians believed that the heart was used during the soul's final judgement.

The body was washed with water, then with palm wine. They packed and covered the body with a natural mineral salt called natron. The body was left to dry in the salt for about 40 days. Bodies were placed on slightly slanted tables to allow the fluids to drain.

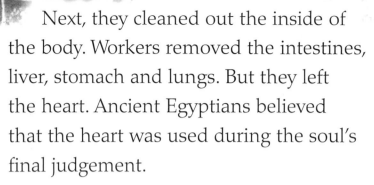

FOUL FACT

Between the 1400s and 1700s, Europeans used mummies as a cure-all medicine. The bodies were ground into powder or mixed with other ingredients and eaten.

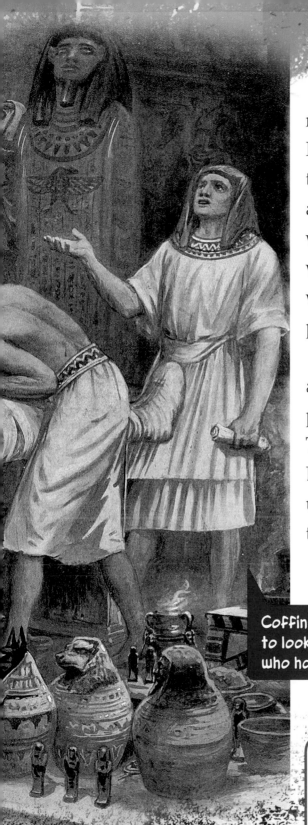

After 40 days, the natron was removed. The body was much lighter. Packing was sometimes stuffed inside the body to make it appear fuller and more lifelike. Finally, the body was washed with perfumed oils and wrapped in **linen** bandages. **Amulets** were placed in the wrappings for protection.

The mummy was then placed in a tomb. During the Old Kingdom, pharaohs' tombs were pyramids. The largest pyramids were at Giza. Later pharaohs preferred hidden, underground tombs. Many of these tombs were in the Valley of the Kings.

Coffins were decorated to look like the person who had died.

linen cloth made from the flax plant
amulet small charm believed to protect the wearer from harm

BREAD AND BAD TEETH

Both rich and poor Egyptians ate a lot of bread. But theirs didn't come presliced from the supermarket. And it could be crunchy! Eating bread in ancient Egypt could mean losing a tooth.

Grain, such as wheat and barley, was the main food product of ancient Egyptian farms. The farms grew so much grain that bread and porridge were the main meals of farmers and labourers. Workers were often paid in grain or loaves of bread.

Bread was made into many different shapes. The dough was sometimes shaped into tall cones, or they could be made into flat disks. Loaves shaped like fish or people have also been found.

Ancient Egyptians liked variety. They flavoured their bread with spices or honey. Ingredients such as dates, eggs, butter and oil added some variety to the bread as well.

BREAD, CIRCA 1500 BC

Grinding flour and making beer was hard, sticky work. Flies were attracted to the sweaty bodies and sweet beer.

Egyptian bread gave a new meaning to wholegrain. Sand from the Sahara desert was everywhere. The sand ended up mixed into the bread flour. The gritty sand was rough on the teeth. Over the years, the sand wore the teeth down and exposed the **nerves**. People with damaged teeth found eating and drinking difficult and painful.

nerve bundle of thin fibres that sends messages between your brain and other parts of your body

Ancient Egyptians also ate a lot of fruit and vegetables. The rich soil by the River Nile made it easy for farmers to grow plenty to eat. Onions and garlic were particular favourites. Meals were washed down with beer and sometimes wine.

Fish and birds that lived in and around the Nile were also part of the standard diet. Other meats were expensive and mostly eaten only by the rich. Ancient Egyptians had no way of refrigerating meat. They had to eat fresh meat quickly or it would spoil. They sometimes preserved meat by drying, smoking or salting it.

No part of the animal went to waste. People ate the ears, brains, hooves and guts. The blood was then boiled and used as a seasoning. Blood was sometimes left to thicken, roasted and eaten as a kind of black pudding.

KEEPING CLEAN

Ancient Egyptians led short lives compared to people today. Many Egyptians died before they were 40. Illness was common. Many women died in childbirth. Injuries also made life risky. Even a small cut or a case of diarrhoea could be deadly.

People in ancient Egypt didn't know about sanitation. Poor disposal of rubbish and bodily waste caused most problems. Rubbish piled up outside houses and in alleys. Flies and other disease-carrying creatures flocked to these areas. The ancient Egyptians did not have sewer systems to carry away waste. Instead, they threw their waste into the Nile and its **canals**. They used this same water for drinking and bathing.

Do you smell that? Then it's time for a bath. Egyptians bathed often, but they did not have soap. Instead, they used natron, the same substance that they used on mummies.

The rich had bathing areas in their houses. The homes of the rich had as many as 10 rooms, so they had space to put in a bathroom. They bathed in bathrooms with tiled floors and painted walls. But poor people only had one-room, mud-brick houses. They bathed in canal or river water.

canal channel dug across land to connect two bodies of water

Bathing in the Nile was dangerous (and not just because of the crocodiles). Tiny pests were always present. People who worked near the water, such as fishermen or brickmakers, were especially vulnerable to the creepy-crawlies. For example, a creature called the guinea worm could enter the human body. It lived under the skin and could grow as long as 1 metre (3 feet). It caused painful blisters and infection.

Early Egyptians used a system of weights and poles to get water from the Nile safely.

Lice were also a problem. Lice can carry disease. They lay their eggs in human hair. Men and women shaved their heads and bodies to rid themselves of lice.

Of course, this doesn't mean that the ancient Egyptians didn't care about hair. In fact, a thick head of black hair was seen as a sign of youth. Like today, women with thinning hair got wigs and hair extensions or tried various recipes to cure baldness. Some recipes included ingredients such as ox blood or donkey liver.

Rich people wore wigs to replace their missing hair. The wigs were made of human hair, sheep's wool or plant fibres.

Something in your eye? The constantly blowing sand, glaring sun and swarms of flies caused many eye infections. There were many blind and nearly blind people.

The desert sand did more than hurt the eyes. People breathed the sand in, causing lung infections and other breathing problems.

FOUL FACT

One recipe for hair tonic involved mixing fat from animals like lions, snakes and hippos. The mixture was then rubbed into the scalp.

Some wigs contained jewellery, flowers and gold strands.

Need the loo? Most Egyptians either relieved themselves outside or into pots. But some rich people had toilets. These toilets had a stone or wooden seat with a hole in it. Below it was a pot that sometimes contained sand. Just like a cat with a litter tray, the user would cover their waste with sand. Of course, these pots had to be emptied. And the contents went to the same place as everything else: the river.

MEDICAL TREATMENTS

Need a doctor? You've come to the right place. Ancient Egyptians had some of the most advanced medicine of their time. But they still had some methods we would find disgusting today.

There were no medical schools, so older doctors trained younger doctors. There were many books that described illnesses and injuries in great detail. The books told the reader what to do in each case, and whether something was curable or not. With this information, doctors could prescribe medicines, set broken bones and treat wounds.

Doctors in ancient Egypt could treat a variety of illnesses.

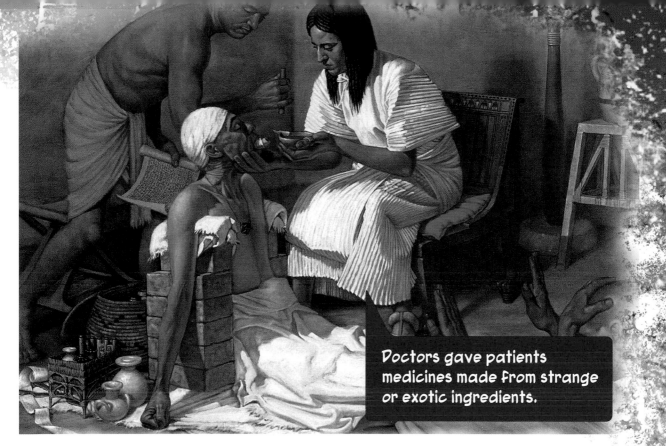

Doctors gave patients medicines made from strange or exotic ingredients.

Many ancient Egyptian cures were practical. For crocodile bites, a doctor would sew up the wound. Many medicines called for honey, which is a natural **bacteria** killer.

Other treatments depended on odd medicines and practices, even magic. Some medicines contained animal dung, urine or blood. One cure called for the patient to sip a special drink made from an onion, honey, water and a mouse's tail. Another remedy called for a mixture of grease and crushed ostrich egg. To try and cure blindness, a doctor would grind up two dried pig's eyes and mix them with honey. He then poured this mixture into the patient's ear.

bacteria microscopic living things

SOLDIERING FOR THE PHARAOH

For most of its history, ancient Egypt did not have a professional army. In times of war, the pharaoh commanded the army. He **conscripted** men as soldiers. Egyptians dreaded going off to war. Being killed and buried away from their homeland was something they feared.

Most ancient Egyptian troops were what's known as foot soldiers. They carried spears, axes and heavy clubs called maces. Long-distance weapons were important too. Archers could attack from a distance with little danger to themselves. Chariots allowed soldiers to fight without getting tired.

Ancient Egyptian soldiers did not have much protection from enemy weapons. They carried shields, but they were made of leather, not metal. The average soldier did not wear armour or a helmet.

Battle wounds were often nasty. A blow with an axe or a mace could cut or smash through bone. An axe could also cut deep into arms and legs, or even take off a limb. Arrows could go through an eye into the brain. A stone from a sling could often crush a skull or cave in a chest.

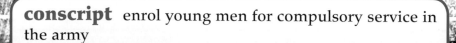

conscript enrol young men for compulsory service in the army

Pharaohs were buried with models of soldiers. The models represented real soldiers and were meant to protect the pharaoh in the afterlife.

Prisoners of war

Slaves in ancient Egypt were often prisoners captured during battles. This ancient text describes prisoners of war in Egypt during the reign of Ramses III.

I gave to them captains of archers, and chief men of the tribes, branded and made into slaves, impressed with my name; their wives and their children were made likewise.

Papyrus Harris, New Kingdom

DOING TIME

Thinking of breaking the law? Think again. The ancient Egyptians did not have a set of written laws. Instead, pharaohs were in charge. Their word was law.

Ancient Egypt did have courts. Most trials were held in local courts. Some trials were held before a royal court. The pharaoh, or his chief adviser, was the judge.

Trials could be harsh affairs. Judges might believe that one side was lying. To get the truth, the judges had these people beaten with sticks.

Ancient Egypt did not have prisons. Instead, criminals would have to pay fines or receive harsh punishments. A common punishment was 100 blows with a stick. Ears and noses might be cut off. Sometimes whole families were punished for the actions of one member.

Murder and treason were punishable by death. Methods of execution included being burnt alive, being impaled on a wooden stake and being eaten by crocodiles.

FOUL FACT

Tomb raiding was the worst crime in ancient Egypt. Punishment was death by torture.

The royal court tried cases involving the death penalty.

Illness, injury and hard work were only a few things that shaped how ancient Egyptians lived. They had a lot to worry about, both in this life and the next!

GLOSSARY

amulet small charm believed to protect the wearer from harm

bacteria microscopic living things

canal channel dug across land to connect two bodies of water

conscript enrol young men for compulsory service in the army

linen cloth made from the flax plant

mummification process of making a mummy to preserve a dead person's body

nerve bundle of thin fibres that sends messages between your brain and other parts of your body

READ MORE

Daily Life in Ancient Egypt (Daily Life in Ancient Civilizations), Don Nardo (Raintree, 2015)

Egyptian Myths and Legends (All About Myths), Fiona Macdonald (Raintree, 2013)

The Egyptian Empire (Great Empires), Ellis Roxburgh (Wayland, 2015)

WEBSITES

ngkids.co.uk/history/ten-facts-about-ancient-egypt
Read facts about Egypt's people, culture, government and history.

www.bbc.co.uk/history/ancient/egyptians
Learn all about pyramids, mummification, pharaohs and the daily life of ancient Egyptians.

INDEX